G000075341

contents

NZ, Canada, US and UK readers

Please note that Australian cup and spoon measurements are metric. A quick conversion guide appears on page 63.

ingredients from a malaysian

bok choy (bak choy, pak choi, chinese white cabbage, chinese chard) mild mustard taste; use stems and leaves. Baby bok choy (at far left) is more tender and delicate in flavour.

bamboo shoots the tender shoots of bamboo plants; available in cans.

banana leaves can be ordered from fruit and vegetable stores. Leaves should be immersed in hot water so they will be pliable.

candlenuts hard, oily, slightly bitter nut, often ground and used to thicken curries. Almonds, macadamias or brazil nuts can be substituted. Refrigerate to prevent nuts from becoming rancid.

chilli, thai red also known as birdseye chillies, these tiny chillies are very hot in flavour and well suited to drying.

chinese rice wine also known as shaoxing wine; replace with a pale dry sherry, if unavailable.

coriander
dried: coriander seeds and ground coriander must never be used to replace fresh coriander, or vice versa, as the tastes are quite different.
fresh: also known as cilantro and chinese parsley, coriander is the herb most often used in Asian cooking.

curry leaves available fresh and dried; buy fresh leaves at Indian food shops. Use leaves to give extra flavour and depth to curries; remove before serving.

fish sauce also called nam pla or nuoc nam; made from pulverised, salted, fermented fish, most often anchovies. Has a pungent smell and strong taste; use sparingly.

galangal fresh galangal looks like ginger but is dense and fibrous and much harder than ginger to cut. Galangal has a distinctive flavour; if using in pieces, remove the galangal from the dish before serving.

garam masala a blend of spices based on varying proportions of cardamom, cinnamon, cloves, coriander. fennel and cumin, roasted and ground together.

ghee clarified butter with the milk solids removed; can be heated to a high temperature without burning.

ginger
fresh: also known as green or root ginger.

pickled: sweet and pink, pickled ginger is available in jars from specialty Asian food stores.

kaffir lime leaves these impart a strong citrus flavour. Leaves are very thick and should be shredded finely and sprinkled over curries or added to salads. Dried leaves are also available; add these to curries.

lemon grass a tall, clumping, lemon-smelling and -tasting, sharp-edged grass; only the white lower part of each stem is used in cooking.

mushrooms, shiitake also known as chinese black mushrooms; fragrant and strongly flavoured, these mushrooms are available dried and fresh. To reconstitute, soak dried mushrooms in hot water for at least 20 minutes before using.

palm sugar also known as jaggery, jawa melaka and gula melaka; from the coconut palm. Dark brown to black in colour; usually sold in rock-hard cakes.

rice stick noodles available in a variety of thicknesses; also known as rice vermicelli. Soak in boiling water to soften for four to eight minutes, but test often because they can quickly turn mushy.

rice, jasmine aromatic long-grain white rice. White rice can be substituted but will not taste the same.

sambal oelek (also ulek or olek) Indonesian in origin; salty paste made from ground chilli.

shallots also known as french shallots, golden shallots or eschalots; small, elongated brown-skinned members of the onion family.

shrimp paste also known as trasi and blachan; a strong-scented, thick, preserved paste made of salted, dried shrimp.

sichuan peppercorns these have a clean, spicy fragrance and slightly lemon flavour; used extensively in Chinese cooking.

star anise a dried star-shaped pod that imparts an astringent aniseed flavour.

tamarind concentrate, thick a purple-black, ready-to-use paste extracted from the pulp of the tamarind bean; used as is, with no soaking, to add a sour flavour.

tofu
firm: this has been pressed slightly; it holds its shape and can be cut into cubes.
fried: small cubes of firm tofu already deep-fried until the surface is brown and crusty and the inside almost dry; can be purchased ready for use.

tomato puree canned pureed tomatoes (not tomato paste).

turmeric a member of the ginger family, this root is dried and ground, resulting in a thick yellow powder. It is pungent in taste but not hot.

vietnamese mint also known as laksa leaf. It is not a true mint and cannot be replaced in recipes with common mint; it has a sharp, pungent taste.

hot and sour soup

1.5kg chicken bones
4 litres (16 cups) water
2 medium brown
    onions (300g),
    chopped coarsely
2 trimmed celery
    sticks (150g),
    chopped coarsely
1 large carrot (180g),
    chopped coarsely
1 tablespoon sichuan
    peppercorns
3 bay leaves
340g chicken breast fillets
6 dried shiitake
    mushrooms
225g can bamboo shoots,
    drained, sliced thinly
10cm piece fresh ginger
    (50g), sliced thinly
2 teaspoons sesame oil
2 tablespoons
    cider vinegar
2 tablespoons sweet
    chilli sauce
¼ cup (60ml) soy sauce
150g rice stick noodles
4 green onions,
    sliced thinly

1 Combine chicken bones with the water, brown onion, celery, carrot, peppercorns and bay leaves in large saucepan. Bring to a boil; simmer, uncovered, 1½ hours, skimming occasionally.

2 Add chicken breast; simmer, uncovered, about 20 minutes or until chicken is cooked through.

3 Strain through muslin-lined strainer into large bowl. Reserve stock and chicken; discard bones and vegetables. When chicken is cool enough to handle, shred finely.

4 Meanwhile, place mushrooms in small heatproof bowl, cover with boiling water, stand 10 minutes; drain. Remove and discard stems from mushrooms; slice caps thinly.

5 Return stock to same cleaned pan with mushrooms, bamboo shoots, ginger, oil, vinegar and sauces; bring to a boil. Simmer, uncovered, 15 minutes, stirring occasionally. Add shredded chicken and noodles; cook, stirring, about 5 minutes or until noodles are just tender.

6 Just before serving, add green onion to soup.

serves 6
per serving 4.5g fat; 686kJ (164 cal)
tip You can use chicken necks or wings to make the stock, rather than the chicken bones.

prawn laksa

1kg medium uncooked prawns
⅓ cup (90g) laksa paste
2¼ cups (560ml) coconut milk
1.25 litres (5 cups) chicken stock
2 red thai chillies, seeded, chopped finely
¼ cup (60ml) lime juice
1 tablespoon brown sugar
6 fresh vietnamese mint leaves, torn
250g rice stick noodles
vegetable oil, for shallow-frying
300g fresh firm tofu, cut into 2cm cubes
2½ cups (200g) bean sprouts
2 green onions, chopped finely

1 Shell and devein prawns, leaving tails intact.
2 Heat large dry saucepan; cook paste, stirring, until fragrant.
3 Stir in milk, stock, chilli, juice, sugar and leaves. Bring to a boil; simmer, uncovered, 30 minutes.
4 Meanwhile, cook noodles in large saucepan of boiling water, uncovered, until just tender; drain. Heat oil in wok or large heavy-based frying pan; cook tofu, in batches, until browned all over. Drain on absorbent paper.
5 Add prawns to laksa mixture; simmer, uncovered, about 5 minutes or until prawns are just changed in colour.
6 Just before serving, add noodles, tofu, sprouts and onion to pan; stir gently until ingredients are just combined and laksa is hot.

serves 4
per serving 48g fat; 3523kJ (843 cal)
tips Don't seed the chillies if you like your laksa hot, or serve it, as they do in Malaysia, with a bowl of sambal oelek.
Omit the prawns in this recipe and substitute chopped, cooked chicken or, for a vegetable version, chopped baby bok choy, spinach or cabbage.

curried lamb pastries

3 cups (450g) plain flour
20g ghee
1 cup (250ml) warm water
1 tablespoon warm water,
    approximately, extra
2 cups (500ml)
    vegetable oil
50g ghee, extra
filling
30g ghee
1 medium brown onion
    (150g), finely chopped
3 cloves garlic, crushed
½ teaspoon sambal oelek
4cm piece fresh ginger
    (20g), grated
1½ tablespoons mild
    curry powder
1 tablespoon
    garam masala
500g lamb mince
2 tablespoons chopped
    fresh coriander
2 tablespoons chopped
    fresh mint
3 eggs, lightly beaten

1 Sift flour into large bowl, rub in ghee. Stir in water and enough extra water to form a soft dough. Turn dough onto lightly floured surface; knead about 10 minutes or until very smooth and elastic.

2 Divide dough into 12 portions; roll each portion into a ball. Place balls in bowl, pour oil over balls; cover, stand 1 hour.

3 Spread a little of the oil over a smooth surface, press out a drained dough ball until a very thin 24cm square.

4 Place ¼ cup of filling in centre of square; spread filling to 10cm square. Fold in sides of dough to form a parcel; trim overlapping edges if too thick. Repeat with remaining dough balls and filling.

5 Heat extra ghee in large heavy-based frying pan; cook parcels until well browned on both sides, drain on absorbent paper. Serve immediately.

filling Heat ghee in large saucepan, add onion, garlic, sambal and ginger; cook, stirring, until onion is soft. Stir in spices; stir until fragrant. Add mince; cook, stirring, until well browned. Stir in herbs, then cool. Stir in eggs.

makes 12
per pastry 17.9g fat; 1388kJ (332 cal)

laksa lemak

There are countless versions of this Malaysian spicy noodle soup, each one delicious. Our recipe features a variety of vegetables but, if you wish, you can add other ingredients, such as prawns or chicken. We used dried rice noodles (also known as rice stick noodles), which are about 5mm wide, in this recipe.

1 litre (4 cups)
  chicken stock
1 cup (250ml) water
⅓ cup (80ml) chilli garlic
  sauce
⅓ cup (80ml) fish sauce
¼ cup (60ml) oyster sauce
1 tablespoon curry powder
400ml coconut cream
250g rice stick noodles
300g baby bok choy,
  trimmed
100g snow peas, halved
200g fresh baby
  corn, halved
150g fried tofu,
  chopped coarsely
3 cups (240g) bean sprouts

1 Combine stock, the water, sauces, curry powder and coconut cream in large saucepan; bring to a boil. Reduce heat; simmer, uncovered, 10 minutes.
2 Meanwhile, place noodles in large heatproof bowl, cover with boiling water, stand until just tender; drain.
3 Add bok choy, snow peas, corn and tofu to stock mixture; cook, uncovered, until vegetables are just tender.
4 Divide noodles among serving bowls; ladle soup into each bowl and top with sprouts.

serves 4
per serving 25.8g fat; 2432kJ (582 cal)
tip You can buy fried tofu from Asian supermarkets or you can cut fresh tofu into cubes and shallow-fry it in vegetable oil until browned lightly.

beef curry puffs

1 tablespoon vegetable oil
1 small brown onion (80g),
    finely chopped
1 small potato (120g),
    finely chopped
2cm piece fresh ginger
    (10g), grated
2 cloves garlic, crushed
4 green onions,
    finely chopped
150g beef mince
1 tablespoon mild
    curry powder
⅓ cup (80ml)
    coconut cream
1½ cups (225g) plain flour
100g butter, chopped
1 egg yolk
2 tablespoons lemon
    juice, approximately
1 egg, lightly beaten

1 Heat oil in large saucepan, add brown onion; cook, stirring, until onion is soft. Add potato, ginger, garlic, green onion and mince; cook, stirring, until mince is browned and potato tender. Add curry powder and cream, mix well; cool.

2 Sift flour into bowl, rub in butter. Add egg yolk and enough juice to form a soft dough. Press dough into a ball, knead gently on lightly floured surface until smooth; cover, refrigerate 30 minutes.

3 Preheat oven to hot. Grease two oven trays. Roll dough between two sheets of baking paper to 3mm thickness. Cut dough into twelve 12cm rounds. Spoon 1½ tablespoons mince mixture onto centre of each round; brush edges with beaten egg. Fold pastry over filling; seal edges with a fork.

4 Place curry puffs on prepared oven trays, brush with remaining beaten egg; bake in hot oven 10 minutes. Reduce heat to moderate; bake further 20 minutes or until browned.

makes 12
per puff 11.9g fat; 811kJ (194 cal)
tips The curry puffs are best cooked just before serving. The mince mixture can be made a day ahead.

spicy fish cakes in banana leaves

Banana leaves need to be ordered from a fruit and vegetable shop or
Asian food store. Usually, one banana leaf can be cut into 10 pieces.
Remove the main stem as it is not suitable to use.

6 fresh kaffir lime
　leaves, chopped
1 stem fresh lemon grass,
　chopped
8 green onions, chopped
1 teaspoon shrimp paste
1 teaspoon grated
　fresh turmeric
3 fresh red thai
　chillies, chopped
½ teaspoon freshly ground
　black pepper
¼ cup firmly packed fresh
　coriander leaves
350g boneless firm white
　fish fillets, chopped
2 eggs, lightly beaten
½ cup (125ml) coconut milk
1 banana leaf
bottled chilli sauce

1 Process lime leaves, lemon grass, onion, paste, turmeric, chilli, pepper and coriander until finely chopped. Add fish; process until just combined.
2 Combine fish mixture and eggs in large bowl; mix well. Gradually stir in coconut milk; mix well.
3 Cut banana leaf into eight 20cm squares. Immerse squares, one at a time, in large saucepan of boiling water; remove immediately, rinse under cold water, then pat dry with absorbent paper. Leaves should be soft and pliable.
4 Place ⅓ cup fish mixture in centre of each square. Lift two sides of leaf and fold towards centre; repeat with other sides to form a parcel. Secure with string.
5 Place parcels, in single layer, in bamboo steamer; cook, covered, over wok or saucepan of boiling water about 10 minutes or until fish mixture is firm. Serve parcels with chilli sauce.

makes 8
per fish cake 4.9g fat; 385kJ (92 cal)
tip This recipe is best made on the day of serving.

beef rendang

2 medium red onions (340g), chopped finely
4 cloves garlic, peeled
4 fresh red thai chillies
4cm piece fresh ginger (20g), grated
5cm stick (10g) fresh lemon grass, chopped finely
1 teaspoon ground turmeric
2 teaspoons ground coriander
1⅔ cups (410ml) coconut milk
1kg beef blade steak, cut into 3cm cubes
1 cinnamon stick
1 tablespoon thick tamarind concentrate
8 curry leaves
1 teaspoon sugar

1 Blend or process onion, garlic, chillies, ginger, lemon grass, turmeric and coriander with ⅓ cup of the coconut milk until smooth.
2 Combine beef, coconut mixture, remaining coconut milk, cinnamon stick, tamarind concentrate and curry leaves in large saucepan; simmer, uncovered, about 1½ hours, stirring occasionally, or until beef is tender.
3 Add sugar; cook stirring, about 15 minutes or until beef is dark and most of the sauce has evaporated.

serves 4
per serving 31.1g fat; 2297kJ (545 cal)
tips This recipe is best made a day ahead and refrigerated, covered; it is also suitable to freeze for up to 3 months.
Beef round steak, skirt steak and gravy beef can be substituted for the blade steak, if preferred.

hainan chicken rice

While named for its Chinese origins, this dish is a firm favourite in
many South-East Asian countries, as well as further afield.

4 single chicken breasts
  on bone (1kg)
1 teaspoon chinese
  rice wine
1 tablespoon soy sauce
2cm piece fresh ginger
  (10g), sliced thinly
1 clove garlic, sliced thinly
2 green onions,
  chopped finely
2 litres (8 cups) water
1 teaspoon sesame oil
¼ teaspoon salt
1 cup (200g) jasmine rice
1 lebanese cucumber
  (130g), sliced thinly
1 green onion, sliced
  thinly, extra
chilli ginger sambal
4 fresh red thai chillies,
  chopped coarsely
1 clove garlic,
  chopped coarsely
2cm piece fresh ginger
  (10g), chopped coarsely
1 teaspoon water
2 teaspoons lime juice

1 Rub chicken all over with combined rice wine
and half of the sauce. Gently slide ginger, garlic and
onion under chicken skin.

2 Bring the water to a boil in large saucepan. Place
chicken in the water. Turn off heat; turn chicken pieces.
Stand chicken in the water 20 minutes; remove chicken
from pan. Return liquid to a boil and repeat this
process another three times.

3 Remove chicken from pan; remove and discard
skin. Brush chicken all over with remaining sauce,
oil and salt.

4 Return cooking liquid to a boil; boil, uncovered,
until reduced by half.

5 Meanwhile, rinse rice thoroughly under cold running
water. Place rice in large saucepan; add enough water
to cover rice by 2cm. Cover pan; bring to a boil. Stir
several times to prevent rice sticking. When boiling,
remove lid and continue to boil until tunnels appear
in rice and all the water has evaporated or been
absorbed; do not stir. Cover rice; stand 20 minutes.
Stir with fork; stand, covered, further 10 minutes.
Cut chicken pieces; serve with rice, cucumber and
chilli ginger sambal. Accompany with a bowl of
cooking liquid sprinkled with extra onion.

chilli ginger sambal Blend ingredients (or grind in
a mortar and pestle) until combined. The sambal can
be made a day ahead and refrigerated, covered.

serves 4
per serving 20.6g fat; 2158kJ (516 cal)

curry kapitan

2 tablespoons
  vegetable oil
2 medium brown onions
  (300g), sliced thinly
¼ cup (60ml) water
1.5kg chicken pieces
2¼ cups (560ml)
  coconut milk
1 cup (250ml)
  coconut cream
spice paste
10 fresh red thai chillies
4 cloves garlic
3cm piece fresh turmeric
  (15g), grated
2cm piece fresh galangal
  (10g), grated
3cm stick (5g) fresh
  lemon grass,
  chopped finely
10 candlenuts
1 tablespoon
  ground cumin
roti jala
1 cup (150g) plain flour
1½ cups (375ml) milk
1 egg

1 Heat oil in wok or large saucepan; cook onion, stirring, until soft. Stir in spice paste and the water; cook, stirring, until fragrant.

2 Add chicken and coconut milk; simmer, covered, 20 minutes. Remove lid; simmer, uncovered, further 30 minutes, stirring occasionally, or until chicken is tender. Stir in coconut cream; serve with roti jala.

spice paste Blend or process ingredients until smooth. (The paste can be made a week ahead and refrigerated, covered.)

roti jala Place flour in large bowl. Gradually stir in combined milk and egg; beat until smooth. Strain batter into jug to remove lumps and make pouring easier. Heat greased 24cm frying pan over medium heat. Pour about ¼ cup of the batter from jug into pan, moving jug back and forth so that pancake will have a lacy appearance. Cook until browned lightly underneath and cooked on top; transfer to greaseproof paper. Stand 1 minute; fold in half. Fold in half again to form a triangle. Repeat with remaining batter.

serves 6
per serving 64.7g fat; 3598kJ (861 cal)
tip The chicken curry and roti jala can be made a day ahead and refrigerated, covered, separately.

dry squid curry

500g squid hoods
2 tablespoons mild chilli powder
1 teaspoon ground turmeric
1 tablespoon thick tamarind concentrate
2 tablespoons hot water
2 tablespoons vegetable oil
2 medium white onions (300g), chopped finely
4 cloves garlic, crushed
2 tablespoons tomato sauce
1 teaspoon soy sauce
1 tablespoon fish sauce
½ teaspoon sugar
⅓ cup (80ml) lemon juice
2 tablespoons packaged fried onions

1 Cut squid into rings. Combine squid, chilli powder and turmeric in large bowl; mix well. Place tamarind concentrate and the water in small bowl.
2 Heat oil in large frying pan; cook squid mixture, stirring, until squid changes colour. Remove from pan.
3 Cook onion and garlic in pan, stirring, until onion is soft. Add tamarind mixture, sauces and sugar; cook, stirring occasionally, 4 minutes.
4 Return squid to pan. Add juice; stir over heat until squid is tender. Serve sprinkled with fried onions.

serves 4
per serving 11.7g fat; 1030kJ (246 cal)
tip This recipe can be made a day ahead and refrigerated, covered.

chicken in tomato coconut sauce

8 chicken drumsticks
½ teaspoon ground turmeric
2 tablespoons vegetable oil
8 green onions, coarsely chopped
2 cloves garlic, coarsely chopped
8cm piece fresh ginger (40g), grated
8 dried red chillies
1 tablespoon vegetable oil, extra
5 cloves
1 star anise
2 cups (500ml) coconut milk
425g can tomato puree
1 cinnamon stick
1 large brown onion (200g), sliced
1 large tomato (250g), sliced
1 cup (125g) frozen peas

1 Using plastic gloves to prevent staining hands, rub chicken with turmeric. Heat oil in large frying pan; cook chicken, in batches, until browned, then drain on absorbent paper.
2 Blend or process green onion, garlic, ginger and chillies until finely chopped.
3 Heat extra oil in pan, add onion mixture, cloves and star anise; cook, stirring, 1 minute. Add coconut milk; simmer, uncovered, 2 minutes.
4 Add chicken, tomato puree and cinnamon; simmer, uncovered, about 10 minutes or until chicken is tender. Stir in onion, tomato and peas; cook, uncovered, about 3 minutes or until peas are tender. Remove cinnamon before serving.

serves 4
per serving 65.4g fat; 3532kJ (845 cal)
tip This recipe can be made a day ahead and stored, covered, in the refrigerator.

prawn sambal

40 medium uncooked prawns (1kg)
1 tablespoon peanut oil
1 large brown onion (200g), chopped finely
2 cloves garlic, crushed
2cm piece fresh ginger (10g), grated
5cm stick (10g) fresh lemon grass, chopped finely
415g can whole peeled tomatoes
1 tablespoon sambal oelek
2 teaspoons lemon juice
1 teaspoon sugar
1 medium red capsicum (200g), chopped finely

1 Shell and devein prawns, leaving tails intact.
2 Heat oil in large frying pan; cook onion, garlic, ginger and lemon grass, stirring, until onion softens.
3 Add undrained crushed tomatoes, sambal, juice, sugar and capsicum; bring to a boil. Reduce heat; simmer, uncovered, until sauce thickens.
4 Add prawns; cook, stirring, until prawns just change colour.
5 Serve sambal with lemon-scented white rice, if desired. Top with shaved lemon rind and green onion curls.

serves 4
per serving 5.8g fat; 875kJ (209 cal)
tip Although this recipe only requires 1 tablespoon of sambal oelek – a salty paste made from ground chillies and vinegar – you can add more for a really fiery treat.

duck with ginger and mushrooms

2.2kg duck
⅓ cup (80ml) soy sauce
6 chinese dried
    mushrooms
vegetable oil,
    for deep-frying
1 tablespoon
    vegetable oil, extra
5cm piece fresh ginger
    (40g), thinly sliced
2 cloves garlic, crushed
1 litre (4 cups) water
1 tablespoon hoisin sauce
1 teaspoon sugar
2 teaspoons sesame oil
¼ teaspoon ground
    black pepper
1 tablespoon tapioca flour
1 tablespoon water, extra
1 tablespoon rice wine
2 green onions,
    sliced thinly

1 Place duck on board, breast-side up. Cut through breastbone, a little to one side, and right through backbone. Cut both pieces of duck in half; discard excess fat and bone.

2 Remove first two bones of wings, discard; cut each breast into six pieces. Cut each thigh and leg into four pieces; discard excess fat.

3 Combine duck and 1 tablespoon of the soy sauce in large bowl, cover; refrigerate 20 minutes. Place mushrooms in small heatproof bowl, cover with boiling water; stand 20 minutes. Drain mushrooms; discard stems, cut caps in half.

4 Heat oil in large saucepan until hot; deep-fry duck, in batches, until browned, then drain on absorbent paper.

5 Heat extra oil in same cleaned pan, add ginger and garlic; cook, stirring, until lightly browned. Add duck, mushrooms, remaining soy sauce, the water, hoisin sauce, sugar, sesame oil and pepper; simmer, uncovered, about 15 minutes or until duck is tender and sauce has reduced to about 2 cups. Add blended flour and extra water; stir over heat until sauce boils and thickens, then stir in wine and onion.

serves 4
per serving 41.1g fat; 2654kJ (635 cal)
tip This recipe can be made a day ahead and stored, covered, in the refrigerator.

fish curry with lemon grass

1kg boneless white fish fillets
¼ cup (60ml) peanut oil
3 large brown onions (600g), sliced thickly
4 cloves garlic, crushed
8cm piece fresh ginger (40g), chopped finely
1 teaspoon ground turmeric
5cm stick (10g) fresh lemon grass, chopped finely
2 tablespoons brown vinegar
1 tablespoon fish sauce
½ cup (125ml) water
2 medium tomatoes (380g), chopped coarsely
2 tablespoons coarsely chopped fresh coriander

1 Cut fish into strips. Heat oil in large frying pan; cook fish, stirring, over medium heat about 1 minute or until fish is cooked slightly. Remove from heat; keep warm.

2 Add onion and garlic to pan; stir over medium heat about 5 minutes or until onion is soft.

3 Stir in ginger, turmeric, lemon grass, vinegar and sauce; bring to a boil. Reduce heat; simmer, uncovered, 3 minutes.

4 Stir in fish and the water; bring to a boil. Reduce heat; simmer, uncovered, about 5 minutes or until fish is tender. Stir in tomato; cook over low heat until mixture is heated through. Stir in coriander.

serves 4
per serving 21.7g fat; 1918kJ (459 cal)

beef stir-fry with ginger and green onion

1 clove garlic, crushed
1 tablespoon cornflour
½ teaspoon bicarbonate of soda
1 egg white
500g beef fillet, sliced thinly
10cm piece fresh ginger (50g), sliced thinly
coarse cooking salt
10 green onions
50g ghee
¼ cup (60ml) water
1 tablespoon oyster sauce

1 Combine garlic, cornflour, soda and egg white in large
bowl, add beef; mix well. Cover; refrigerate 30 minutes.
2 Combine ginger and salt in small bowl, cover; stand
20 minutes. Rinse ginger under water, drain; pat dry
with absorbent paper.
3 Cut onions into 5cm lengths. Heat ghee in wok or large
heavy-based frying pan until very hot, add onion and ginger;
cook, stirring, over high heat 1 minute. Remove from wok.
4 Reheat same wok, add beef mixture and the water;
cook, stirring, over high heat until beef is just tender.
Add onion, ginger and oyster sauce; cook, stirring,
until heated through.

serves 4
per serving 20.2g fat; 1304kJ (312 cal)

spicy coconut chicken

Ayam percik, as it is known in Kelantan, Malaysia, features chicken pieces marinated in a spicy coconut sauce then grilled over coals, but it also suits oven cooking.

1 tablespoon ground coriander
1 tablespoon ground cumin
1 tablespoon fennel seeds
1 teaspoon ground turmeric
2 fresh red thai chillies, seeded, chopped finely
½ teaspoon tamarind concentrate
2 cloves garlic, crushed
1 tablespoon finely chopped fresh lemon grass
2 teaspoons palm sugar
1 tablespoon peanut oil
½ cup (125ml) coconut cream
8 chicken thigh cutlets (1.2kg)

1 Preheat oven to hot.
2 Combine spices, chilli, tamarind, garlic, lemon grass, sugar, oil and coconut cream in large bowl; stir until mixture forms a paste.
3 Add chicken to bowl; stir to coat in paste. Place chicken on wire rack in large shallow baking dish. Bake in hot oven about 15 minutes. Cover with foil; bake about 20 minutes or until chicken is cooked through.

serves 4
per serving 27g fat; 1760kJ (421 cal)
tip To allow the flavours to develop, marinate the chicken overnight; store, covered, in the refrigerator.

swordfish curry

Shallots, also called french shallots, golden shallots or eschalots, are small, elongated members of the onion family that grow in tight clusters, similarly to garlic. You need approximately 2 sticks fresh lemon grass for this recipe.

6 fresh red thai chillies,
  chopped coarsely
2 cloves garlic, quartered
10 shallots (120g),
  chopped coarsely
½ cup coarsely chopped
  fresh lemon grass
5cm piece galangal (25g),
  quartered
1 teaspoon curry powder
1 teaspoon ground
  coriander
¼ teaspoon ground
  turmeric
2 tablespoons
  vegetable oil
1 tablespoon fish sauce
1⅔ cups (400ml)
  coconut milk
1⅔ cups (400ml)
  coconut cream
2 cups (400g) jasmine rice
4 x 220g swordfish
  steaks, skinned
¼ cup (10g) flaked
  coconut, toasted
4 kaffir lime leaves,
  shredded finely

1 Blend or process chilli, garlic, shallot, lemon grass, galangal, curry powder, coriander, turmeric and half of the oil until mixture forms a paste.

2 Heat remaining oil in large frying pan; cook paste, stirring, over medium heat about 3 minutes or until fragrant. Add sauce, coconut milk and cream; bring to a boil. Reduce heat; simmer, uncovered, about 15 minutes or until mixture thickens slightly.

3 Meanwhile, cook rice in large saucepan of boiling water, uncovered, until tender; drain. Cover to keep warm.

4 Cook swordfish on heated oiled grill plate (or grill or barbecue), in batches, until browned both sides and cooked as desired.

5 Divide fish among serving bowls; top with sauce, sprinkle with toasted coconut and lime leaves. Serve rice in separate bowls.

serves 4
per serving 59.5g fat; 4667kJ (1115 cal)
tip If you can't find shallots, substitute a medium brown onion and a small clove of crushed garlic.

mutton and potato curry

½ cup firmly packed fresh coriander leaves
4 cloves garlic, chopped coarsely
6 green onions, chopped coarsely
8cm piece fresh galangal (40g), grated
8cm piece fresh ginger (40g), grated
1kg diced mutton
2 tablespoons vegetable oil
2 large brown onions (400g), sliced thinly
¼ teaspoon ground cardamom
6 cloves
½ teaspoon ground fennel
1 teaspoon ground turmeric
½ teaspoon ground cumin
2 cups (500ml) coconut milk
400g baby new potatoes, halved
2 tablespoons packaged ground almonds

1 Blend or process coriander, garlic, green onion, galangal and ginger
until well combined. Combine mutton and coriander mixture in large bowl;
mix well. Cover; refrigerate several hours or overnight.
2 Preheat oven to moderately slow. Heat half of the oil in large ovenproof dish;
cook mutton, in batches, until well browned all over. Remove from pan.
3 Heat remaining oil in same dish, add brown onion; cook, stirring, until soft.
Add cardamom, cloves, fennel, turmeric and cumin; cook, stirring, 2 minutes.
4 Return mutton to dish, add coconut milk; simmer, uncovered, 3 minutes.
Cover with foil. Bake in moderately slow oven 1 hour. Add potatoes; bake
further 1 hour or until mutton and potatoes are tender. Add nuts; cook,
stirring, until heated through.

serves 6
per serving 39.9g fat; 2420kJ (579 cal)
tip This recipe is best made just before serving.

stir-fried silverbeet and almonds

2 teaspoons peanut oil
⅓ cup (25g) flaked almonds
2 tablespoons sweet sherry
2 tablespoons soy sauce
2 tablespoons honey
1 clove garlic, crushed
½ teaspoon sesame oil
1kg silverbeet, trimmed
6 green onions, chopped coarsely

1 Heat peanut oil in heated large wok or frying pan. Stir-fry nuts until just browned; remove from wok. Cook sherry, sauce, honey, garlic and oil in wok until sauce boils.
2 Add silverbeet and onion; stir-fry, tossing until silverbeet just wilts. Serve silverbeet mixture with nuts sprinkled over the top.

serves 4
per serving 5.3g fat; 626kJ (150 cal)

mango sambal

1 teaspoon shrimp paste
1 large mango (600g), peeled
1 fresh red thai chilli, chopped finely
1 teaspoon sugar
½ teaspoon soy sauce

1 Cook paste in small dry non-stick saucepan until dry and crumbly.
2 Cut mango into 1cm cubes. Combine paste, mango, chilli, sugar and sauce in medium bowl; mix well.

makes 1½ cups
per ½ cup 0.4g fat; 371kJ (89 cal)
tip This recipe can be made a day ahead and refrigerated, covered.

cucumber and pineapple sambal

3 teaspoons shrimp paste
2 fresh red thai chillies, seeded, chopped finely
1 tablespoon lime juice
1 tablespoon soy sauce
1 teaspoon sugar
1 small green cucumber (130g), peeled, seeded, chopped coarsely
1 small pineapple (800g), chopped coarsely
6 green onions, sliced thinly

1 Cook paste in dry large saucepan until dry and crumbly. Combine paste and chilli in small bowl; grind with mortar and pestle. Stir in juice, sauce and sugar; mix well.
2 Combine cucumber, pineapple and onion in large bowl; stir in chilli mixture.

serves 6
per serving 0.3g fat; 230kJ (55 cal)
tip This recipe can be made a day ahead and refrigerated, covered.

spicy okra

5 shallots, halved
1 fresh red thai chilli, chopped coarsely
2 cloves garlic, halved
1 teaspoon shrimp paste
20g ghee
450g okra, halved
¾ cup (180ml) milk
½ cup (75g) plain flour
60g ghee, extra

1 Blend or process shallots, chilli, garlic and paste until finely chopped. Heat ghee in large frying pan or wok, add shallot mixture; cook, stirring, until fragrant. Remove from pan.
2 Combine okra and milk in large bowl, drain; discard milk. Toss okra in flour. Heat extra ghee in pan; cook okra, in batches, until lightly browned. Drain on absorbent paper.
3 Combine okra and shallot mixture in large bowl; mix well.

serves 6
per serving 14.9g fat; 849kJ (203 cal)
tip This recipe is best made just before serving.

eggplant and shrimp sambal

⅓ cup (40g) dried shrimp
1 medium brown onion (150g), chopped coarsely
2 green onions, chopped coarsely
2 cloves garlic, halved
2 teaspoons chilli powder
2 teaspoons white vinegar
2 teaspoons sugar
¼ cup (60ml) water
1 tablespoon vegetable oil
2 teaspoons sesame oil
2 medium eggplant (600g)
vegetable oil, for deep-frying, extra

1 Place shrimp in small heatproof bowl; cover with boiling water. Stand about 10 minutes or until soft; drain. Blend or process shrimp, brown onion, green onion, garlic, chilli, vinegar, sugar and the water until chopped finely.
2 Heat vegetable oil and sesame oil in small frying pan, add shrimp mixture; cook, stirring, about 2 minutes or until fragrant.
3 Cut eggplant into 1cm-thick slices; heat extra oil in large saucepan. Deep-fry eggplant, in batches, until browned lightly; drain on absorbent paper. Top warm eggplant slices with shrimp mixture.

serves 8
per serving 7.8g fat; 412kJ (99 cal)

roti canai

3 cups (450g) plain flour
1 teaspoon sugar
1 egg
¾ cup (180ml) warm water, approximately
100g ghee, melted, approximately

1 Combine flour and sugar in large bowl; stir in egg and enough of the water to mix to a soft dough. Turn dough onto lightly floured surface; knead about 10 minutes or until smooth and elastic. Cover dough with plastic wrap; stand 2 hours.

2 Divide dough into 12 portions. Roll one portion on lightly floured surface to form 18cm circle. Brush circle with a little of the ghee. Roll dough up tightly like a swiss roll, then roll up both ends so they meet in the centre. Repeat with remaining dough portions. While working with dough, keep other portions covered with plastic wrap to prevent them from drying out. If making ahead, brush rolls with a little of the ghee; cover with plastic wrap.

3 Roll out rolls on lightly floured surface into 17cm circles. Cook roti over high heat in large heavy-based frying pan greased with ghee, until puffed and browned lightly on both sides.

makes 12
per serving 9.2g fat; 885kJ (212 cal)

char kway teow

This classic Malaysian fried noodle dish is best made with fresh noodles.

1kg fresh rice noodles
500g small uncooked prawns
2 tablespoons peanut oil
340g chicken breast fillets, chopped coarsely
4 fresh red thai chillies, seeded, chopped finely
2 cloves garlic, crushed
2cm piece fresh ginger (10g), grated
5 green onions, sliced thinly
2 cups (160g) bean sprouts
⅓ cup (80ml) soy sauce
¼ teaspoon sesame oil
1 teaspoon brown sugar

1 Place noodles in large heatproof bowl, cover with boiling water; gently separate with fork, drain.
2 Shell and devein prawns, leaving tails intact; halve prawns crossways.
3 Heat half of the peanut oil in wok or large frying pan; stir-fry chicken, chilli, garlic and ginger until chicken is cooked through. Remove from wok.
4 Heat remaining peanut oil in wok; stir-fry prawns until they just change colour. Remove from wok. Stir-fry onion and sprouts in wok until onion is soft. Add noodles and combined remaining ingredients; stir-fry 1 minute.
5 Return chicken mixture and prawns to wok; stir-fry until heated through.

serves 6
per serving 10.4g fat; 1464kJ (350 cal)
tip Char kway teow is best made just before serving.

chicken satay noodles

2 teaspoons ground
  coriander
2 teaspoons ground cumin
2 teaspoons ground
  turmeric
700g chicken thigh fillets,
  chopped coarsely
250g hokkien noodles
6 green onions
150g fresh baby corn
2 tablespoons peanut oil
1 large carrot (180g),
  sliced thinly
2 tablespoons
  finely chopped
  fresh coriander
satay sauce
½ cup (130g) crunchy
  peanut butter
½ cup (125ml)
  coconut cream
½ cup (125ml)
  chicken stock
2 tablespoons sweet
  chilli sauce
2 tablespoons soy sauce
1 tablespoon brown sugar
1 tablespoon lime juice

1 Combine ground coriander, cumin and turmeric in medium bowl. Add chicken; mix well to coat with spices.

2 Rinse noodles under hot running water; drain. Transfer to large bowl; separate noodles with fork.

3 Chop onions and corn diagonally into 4cm pieces.

4 Heat half of the oil in heated large wok or frying pan; stir-fry chicken mixture, in batches, until browned.

5 Heat remaining oil in wok; stir-fry corn and carrot until just tender. Return chicken to wok with noodles, onion and satay sauce; stir-fry until heated through. Sprinkle with fresh coriander.

satay sauce Combine ingredients in medium jug; whisk until combined.

serves 4

per serving 45.6g fat; 2753kJ (659 cal)

tip Bottled satay sauce can be substituted for the satay sauce, and rice or egg noodles can be substituted for hokkien noodles, if preferred.

coconut milk rice

Serve this dish hot, as an accompaniment.

1½ cups (300g) long-grain rice
1½ cups (375ml) water
1½ cups (375ml) coconut milk
3 green onions, chopped
4cm piece fresh ginger (20g), grated

1 Rinse rice in strainer under cold water until water runs clear.
2 Combine rice, the water and coconut milk in large heavy-based saucepan; bring to a boil, stirring, then simmer gently, covered, 15 minutes. Remove from heat; stand, covered, on damp tea-towel 10 minutes. It is important not to remove lid while cooking and steaming.
3 Fluff rice with a fork; gently stir through onion and ginger.

serves 4
per serving 19.4g fat; 1902kJ (455 cal)
tip This recipe can be made a day ahead and stored, covered, in the refrigerator.

mee goreng

Kecap manis is Indonesian thick soy sauce which has sugar and spices added.

600g hokkien noodles
2 tablespoons
    vegetable oil
2 cloves garlic, crushed
2cm piece fresh ginger
    (10g), grated
3 kaffir lime leaves,
    chopped finely
1 large red capsicum
    (350g), sliced thinly
1 bunch baby
    bok choy (500g),
    chopped coarsely
6 green onions,
    chopped coarsely
1 cup (80g) bean sprouts
1 teaspoon cornflour
⅓ cup (80ml) kecap manis
2 tablespoons sweet
    chilli sauce
1 teaspoon sesame oil
1 tablespoon water

1 Place noodles in large heatproof bowl, cover with boiling water; stand until just tender, drain.

2 Meanwhile, heat vegetable oil in wok or large frying pan; stir-fry garlic, ginger, lime leaves, capsicum and bok choy 2 minutes or until vegetables are almost tender.

3 Add onion, sprouts and noodles; stir to combine. Blend cornflour with kecap manis, sauce, sesame oil and the water, add to wok; cook, stirring, until mixture boils and thickens slightly.

serves 4
per serving 11.5g fat; 1355kJ (324 cal)
tip You could substitute chinese cabbage or any other Asian green for the baby bok choy if it's not available.

tomato rice

Serve this dish hot, as an accompaniment.

125g ghee
8 shallots, sliced thinly
1 medium onion (150g), chopped finely
2 cloves garlic, crushed
¼ cup (50g) candlenuts, chopped finely
2 cinnamon sticks
2 star anise
2 cloves
2 cups (400g) white long-grain rice
3 cups (750ml) boiling water
⅓ cup (90g) tomato paste

1 Heat half of the ghee in large heavy-based frying pan, add shallots; cook, stirring, until lightly browned and crisp. Drain on absorbent paper. Heat remaining ghee in same pan, add onion, garlic, candlenuts, cinnamon sticks, star anise and cloves; cook, stirring, until onion is soft.

2 Stir in rice, the water and paste; simmer gently, covered, 15 minutes. Remove from heat; stand, covered, on damp tea-towel 10 minutes.

3 Fluff rice with a fork. Discard spices; serve topped with shallots.

serves 6
per serving 21.4g fat; 1902kJ (455 cal)
tip It is important not to remove the lid while cooking and steaming the rice.

index

facts & figures

These conversions are approximate only, but the difference between an exact and the approximate conversion of various liquid and dry measures is minimal and will not affect your cooking results.

Note: NZ, Canada, US and UK all use 15ml tablespoons. Australian tablespoons measure 20ml. All cup and spoon measurements are level.

Measuring equipment
The difference between one country's measuring cups and another's is, at most, within a 2 or 3 teaspoon variance. (For the record, 1 Australian metric measuring cup holds approximately 250ml.) The most accurate way of measuring dry ingredients is to weigh them. For liquids, use a clear glass or plastic jug having metric markings.

How to measure
When using graduated measuring cups, shake dry ingredients loosely into the appropriate cup. Do not tap the cup on a bench or tightly pack the ingredients unless directed to do so. Level the top of measuring cups and measuring spoons with a knife. When measuring liquids, place a clear glass or plastic jug having metric markings on a flat surface to check accuracy at eye level.

Dry measures

metric	imperial
15g	½oz
30g	1oz
60g	2oz
90g	3oz
125g	4oz (¼lb)
155g	5oz
185g	6oz
220g	7oz
250g	8oz (½lb)
280g	9oz
315g	10oz
345g	11oz
375g	12oz (¾lb)
410g	13oz
440g	14oz
470g	15oz
500g	16oz (1lb)
750g	24oz (1½lb)
1kg	32oz (2lb)

We use large eggs with an average weight of 60g.

Liquid measures

metric	imperial
30 ml	1 fluid oz
60 ml	2 fluid oz
100 ml	3 fluid oz
125 ml	4 fluid oz
150 ml	5 fluid oz (¼ pint/1 gill)
190 ml	6 fluid oz
250 ml (1cup)	8 fluid oz
300 ml	10 fluid oz (½ pint)
500 ml	16 fluid oz
600 ml	20 fluid oz (1 pint)
1000 ml (1litre)	1¾ pints

Helpful measures

metric	imperial
3mm	⅛in
6mm	¼in
1cm	½in
2cm	¾in
2.5cm	1in
6cm	2½in
8cm	3in
20cm	8in
23cm	9in
25cm	10in
30cm	12in (1ft)

Oven temperatures
These oven temperatures are only a guide for conventional ovens. For fan-forced ovens, check the manufacturer's manual.

	°C (Celsius)	°F (Fahrenheit)	Gas Mark
Very slow	120	250	½
Slow	150	275 – 300	1 – 2
Moderately slow	160	325	3
Moderate	180	350 – 375	4 – 5
Moderately hot	200	400	6
Hot	220	425 – 450	7 – 8
Very hot	240	475	9

Reprinted in 2011 by Octopus Publishing Group Limited based on
materials licensed to it by ACP Magazines Ltd, a division of PBL Media Pty Limited

54 Park St, Sydney
GPO Box 4088, Sydney, NSW 2001
phone (02) 9282 8618; fax (02) 9267 9438
acpbooks@acpmagazines.com.au; www.acpbooks.com.au

ACP BOOKS

General manager Christine Whiston
Editor-in-chief Susan Tomnay
Creative director Hieu Chi Nguyen
Art director Hannah Blackmore
Designer Sarah Holmes
Senior editor Wendy Bryant
Food director Pamela Clark

Published and Distributed in the United Kingdom by Octopus Publishing Group Limited
Endeavour House
189 Shaftesbury Avenue
London WC2H 8JY
United Kingdom
phone + 44 (0) 207 632 5400; fax + 44 (0) 207 632 5405
aww@octopusbooks.co.uk; www.octopusbooks.co.uk
www.australian-womens-weekly.com

Printed and bound in China.

A catalogue record for this book is available from the British Library.
ISBN 978-1-863964-98-2
First published by ACP Magazines Ltd in 2005
© ACP Magazines Ltd 2005

ABN 18 053 273 546
To order books:
telephone LBS on 01903 828 503
order online at www.australian-womens-weekly.com
or www.octopusbooks.co.uk

Send recipe enquiries to: recipeenquiries@acpmagazines.com.au